Mom....
Merry Christmas
2006!
Love Julie

Above the North

Charlevoix

Above the North

AERIAL PHOTOGRAPHY OF NORTHERN MICHIGAN BY MARGE BEAVER

University of Michigan Press
Ann Arbor
&
Petoskey Publishing Company
Traverse City

Published in the United States of America by

The University of Michigan Press

&

The Petoskey Publishing Company

Manufactured in Canada by Friesens

2009 2008 2007 2006 4 3 2 1

ISBN-13: 978-0-472-11549-5 (cloth : alk. paper)

ISBN-10: 0-472-11549-9 (cloth : alk. paper)

Library of Congress Cataloging in Publication Data on file

INTRODUCTION

Marge Beaver bought her first plane in 1982 to meld her two passions, flying and photography. Now, after 25 years and close to 7000 hours later as pilot and photographer, she still thoroughly enjoys trying to produce those amazing images that just aren't normally seen. A slumping winter dune at Sleeping Bear, a path cut through the ice and underneath the Mackinac Bridge, fall colors that take your breath away and amazing blues, greens and whites along our shoreline—images that make you pause in amazement as you study the photographs in more detail. As you look through the pages, you will see that Marge Beaver's love of how Michigan looks from the air shows in her photos.

Marge is someone of few words, unless of course you subscribe to the belief, "A picture is worth a thousand words." If so, Marge Beaver's work speaks volumes.

"I have flown all over the country for hundreds of customers, taking pictures in nearly every state, and Michigan is still my favorite place to live, fly and photograph. It just doesn't get any better; the lakes, the dunes, the harbors, the forests; we have it all, and I am excited to share the incredible views I get to see when I am flying.

"One of the special things about doing this book is that I was offered an excuse to try and be even more artistic with the photographs, capturing the lakes and rivers and orchards, ice flows and even a simple view of hay bailing that I hope will give the moments pause, or even longer, to appreciate our great state."

The Glory
When you are flying over clouds when the sun is shining, looking out the window in the right direction, you will see the shadow of the airplane on the clouds, surrounded by a "rainbow" circle. It is what nearly every pilot has seen, and hopefully, someday you will, too.

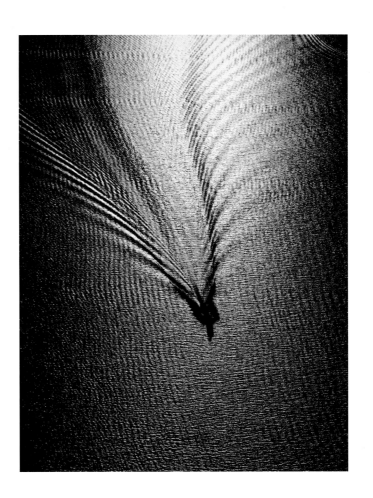

Boat on Lake Charlevoix

South Manitou Island

Frankfort Lighthouse

Torch Lake

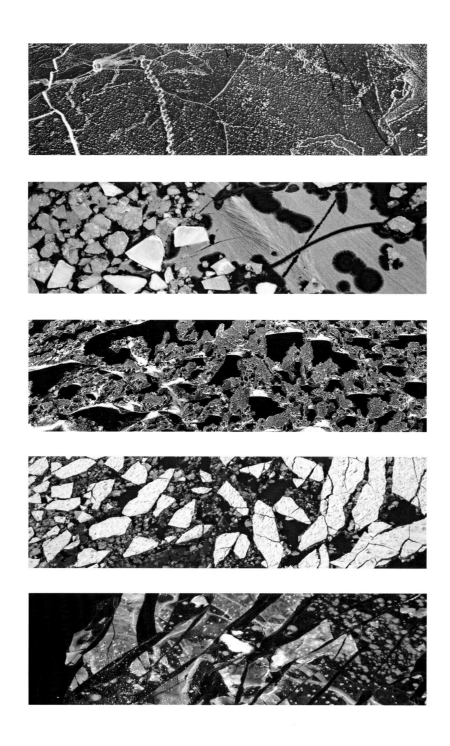

Ice on Lake Michigan

River Oxbows

Mackinaw City wind turbines

Long Lake sunset

New Presque Isle Lighthouse

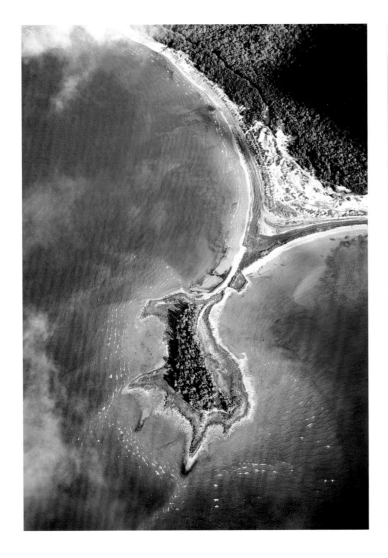

Fisherman's Island

Onekama

Grand Traverse Resort

Ludington

Ludington State Park

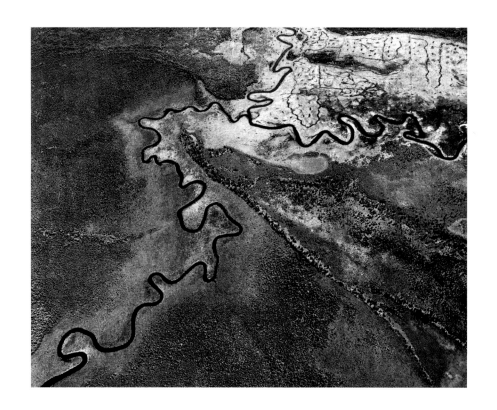

Dead Stream Swamp

Au Sable River

Orchard in spring

Orchard with snow

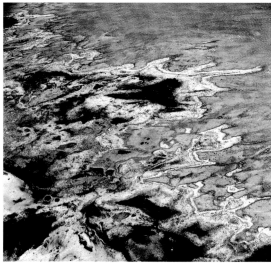

Rogers City Harbor

Sand shallows

Peninsula in Houghton Lake

Old Presque Isle Lighthouse

Mackinac Bridge

The Grand Hotel on Mackinac Island

Clear cut squares

Fall color on Manistee River

Cheboygan Lighthouse

Hamlin Lake sand & boats

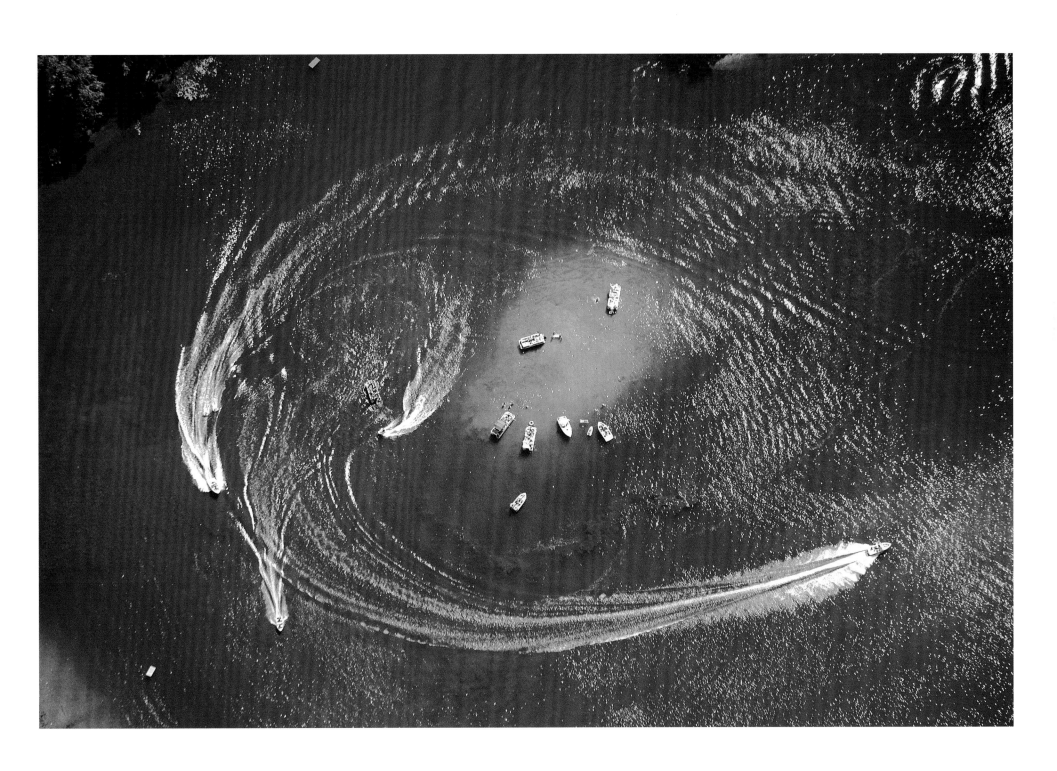

Boating fun

Wilderness State Park

Round Island Lighthouse

Sand dune

Shoreline south of Leland

Hay bales

Harvest time

Glen Lake sunset

Fall color west of Cadillac

Mackinac Bridge

Harbor Springs in the fall

Quarry at Stoneport

Suttons Bay

Grand Traverse Lighthouse

Ice flows in Lake Michigan

Middle Island Lighthouse

Clam Lake & Lake Bellaire

Wilderness State Park

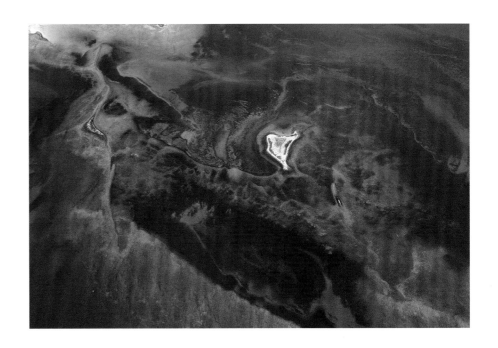

Garden Isle

Lake Leelanau

Little Traverse Lighthouse

Sleeping Bear Dunes in the winter

Island in the Au Sable River

Beaver Island

Houghton Lake

Bois Blanc Island

Sturgeon Point Lighthouse

Ile Aux Galets

Frankfort Harbor in fog

Oil barge in Grand Traverse Bay

Lansing Shoal Lighthouse

Walloon Lake

Big Sable Lighthouse

Thunder Bay Island Lighthouse

St. Helena Island

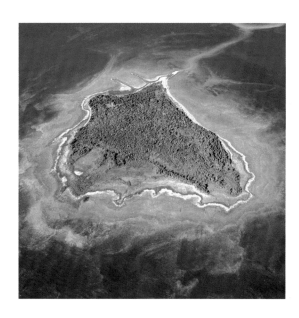

Squaw Island

Rogers City

Tawas Point

Whiskey Island

North Fox Island

Mackinac Island

South Fox Island

Old Mission Peninsula

North Manitou Island

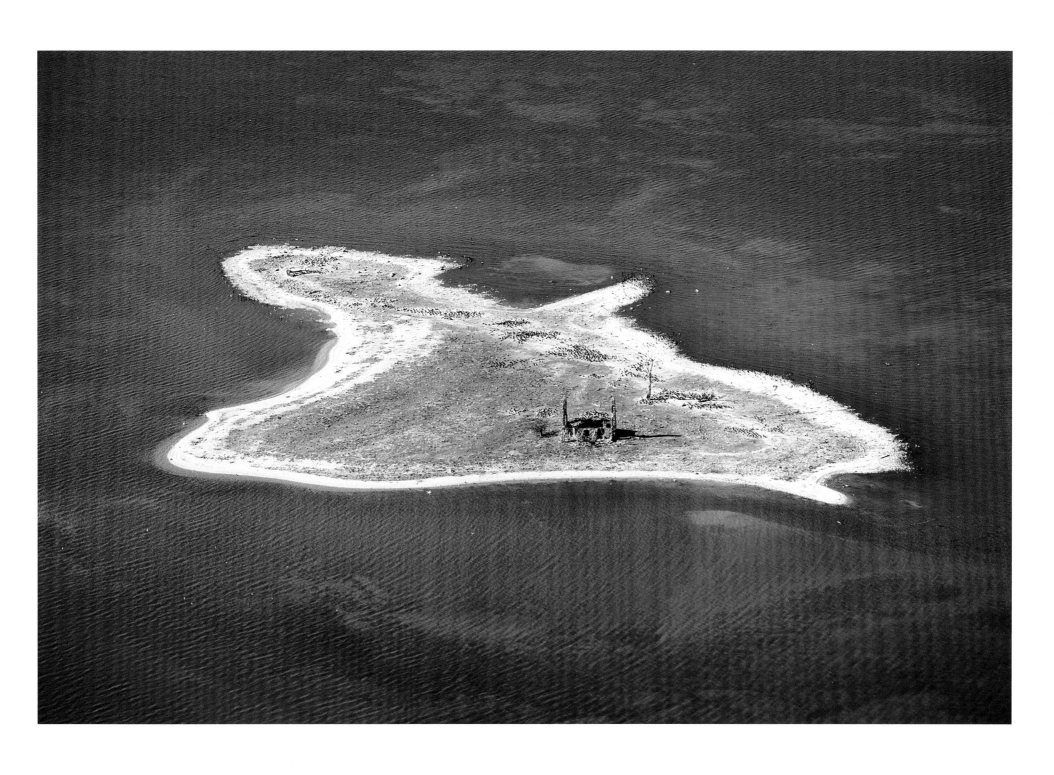

Gull Island

Arcadia shoreline

40 Mile Point Lighthouse

Grand Traverse Bay

Stoney Point

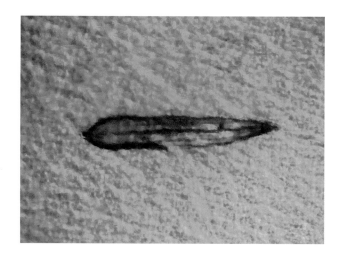

Shipwreck remains

South Manitou Island

Platte Lake sunset

Ludington sunset

Power Island sunset

Manistee sunset

Frankfort sunset

Crystal Lake

Clouds over the shoreline

Thunder Bay Island

Empire Bluffs

Sand & trees

Manistee historical view

Manistee in the fall

Elk Rapids

Bay Harbor

Little Traverse Bay Lighthouse

Glen Lake

Point Betsie Lighthouse

Presque Isle Harbor

The Meribeth Andrie

Harrisville Harbor

Point Betsie Lighthouse

Boyne City

Charlevoix

Manistee sunset

Higgins Lake

Acme

Leland

Algae on an inland lake

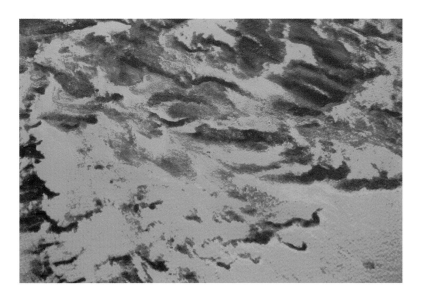

Water patterns

Bass Lake & Long Lake

Stoneport

Acme

South Manitou Island Lighthouse

Manistee River in the fall

Portage Lake & Lake Michigan

Mackinac Bridge

Platte River

Tawas

Michigan inland waterway

Waugoshance Lighthouse

Water patterns

Round Island Lighthouse

Pyramid Point

Frankfort sunset

Arcadia Bluffs

Mackinac Bridge

Grelickville

Hog Island

Garden Isle

Grand Traverse Bay

Mackinac Island

Charlevoix

Hemingway Point

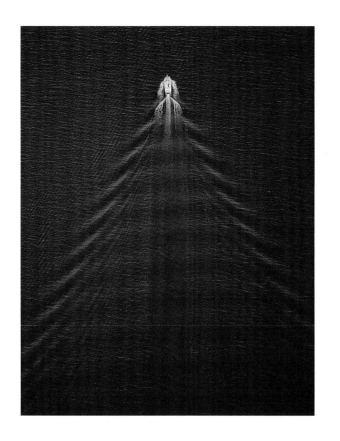